Animals Two by Two

Developed at
Lawrence Hall of Science
University of California at Berkeley

Published and Distributed by **Delta Education**

1-58356-887-5

542-2040

2 3 4 5 6 7 8 9 10 SPC 09 08 07 06 05 04

Table of Contents

Learning about Animals

Animals come in many sizes.
Animals live in many places.
You can learn about animals by
looking at them closely.

Goldfish and Guppies

Where do you find fish?
Some fish live in fresh water.
Some fish live in salt water.
Fish find food in the water.

Fish have eyes, scales, a mouth, and fins.
Do you see them?

Fish have gills, too.
All fish breathe through gills.

How are these fish the same?
How are they different?

Land and Water Snails

Where do you find snails?
Some snails live in water.
Some snails live on land
in moist places.

Snails have tentacles and a foot.
Do you see them?
What else do you see?

All snails have a mouth.
Snails scrape food into their
mouths.

How are these snails the same?
How are they different?

Big and Little Worms

Where do you find worms?
These worms live in the soil.
They get water and food
from the soil.

Grown-up earthworms have
a clitellum.
Do you see it?
What else do you see?

These worms have segments.

How are these worms the same?
How are they different?

Isopods

Where do you find isopods?
These isopods live on land.
Look for them under leaves and
rocks where it is moist.

Isopods have antennae and legs.
Do you see them?
What else do you see?

All isopods breathe with gills.

How are these isopods the same?
How are they different?

Eggs and Chicks

Where do you find birds?
Where do birds find
food to eat and water to drink?

Birds have feathers and wings.
Do you see them?
What else do you see?

Female birds lay eggs.
Baby birds hatch out of
the eggs.

How are these birds the same?
How are they different?

Which animals go together two by two?
Why do you think so?